Concepts
FOR TIMPANI
BY JOHN BECK

CARL FISCHER®
65 Bleecker Street, New York, NY 10012

O5486

ISBN 0-8258-4142-9

Concepts

FOR TIMPANI
BY JOHN BECK

Foreword

CONCEPTS FOR TIMPANI is the result of my many years of playing and teaching timpani. The contents of this book reflect a natural approach to the instrument. An approach, that if perfected, will produce a quality sound that will blend with music and at the same time cause the performer to remain relaxed regardless of the technical difficulty.

Throughout history, timpani have been a part of the musical heritage of the great composers: Haydn, Handel, Beethoven, Brahms, Dvořak, Tchaikovsky, Berlioz, Bartók and Strauss to name a few. Each one demanded something different from the timpani; however, each one wanted to hear or expected to hear quality.

CONCEPTS FOR TIMPANI assumes the percussionist has already developed basic music skills including an understanding of rhythms, dynamics, tempos, and other musical symbols. The material within deals with the quality sound from the early stages of development to the professional stage. It is a book for the beginner, intermediate or advanced student. Exercises, etudes and solos of all difficulties provide the student with ample material to practice. It is not necessary to progress from page to page when using the book but seek out the desired section and work on it, then move to another section. Once each technical concept is understood in all the sections, a complete timpanist will be developed.

It is my intention to provide the timpanist with the knowledge that has enabled me to enjoy a musical career playing and teaching timpani. I am confident that CONCEPTS FOR TIMPANI will do that. I hope you enjoy the concepts.

— John H. Beck

Professor of Percussion, Eastman School of Music

Timpanist, Rochester Philharmonic Orchestra

Acknowledgements

My teacher William G. Street, Professor of Percussion, Eastman School of Music & Timpanist of the Rochester Philharmonic Orchestra (deceased).

My former and present students who, over these past forty-two years, have helped shape my technique and ideas.

My daughter Laurie J. Beck, for her photography.

History of the Timpani

Unlike other instruments of the percussion family, the timpani needs to be understood historically before a true playing concept can be attained. Whether the instrument is called **TIMPANO** (singular) **or TIMPANI** (plural)- (Italian), **TYMPANI** (a misspelling), **KETTLEDRUMS** (English), **PAUKEN** (German), **TIMBALES** (French) **or TIMBALS** (Spanish), the historical lineage is long and well documented.

The first appearance of timpani in western Europe occurred in the fifteenth century as cavalry instruments used by the Muslims, Ottoman Turks and Mongols. In 1457, a procession consisting of over 500 people and 700 horses representing King Ladislas V of Hungary, marched into Paris. Many of the horses carried large cauldron-like drums, an unusual spectacle for the time. The fame of these mounted drums spread throughout Europe via the courts of German speaking lands. They were soon paired with trumpets and became the exclusive possession of the court which they represented. During the fifteenth and sixteenth centuries, the employment of both trumpeters and timpanists was restricted to emperors, kings, electors, dukes, princes, counts, lords, and others of high rank. Secret guilds of trumpeters and timpanists were formed whose members were forbidden to associate with other instrumentalists who were considered to be mere household employees of inferior rank. In the seventeenth century, timpani found their way indoors, joining the orchestra along with the trumpets, horns, and oboes. In 1670, timpani were introduced in large liturgical pieces and court orchestral operatic ensembles. From this point in history to the present, timpani have been used by composers of all styles of music.

The Role Of The Timpanist

Since the beginning of timpani history, timpanists have held a regal position. From their initial use as cavalry instruments to their position in the courts of Europe and their elite guilds and finally to their central position in the orchestra or band, the timpani and timpanist alike have assumed a role of responsibility both historically and musically. To fully accept this responsibility is to perform in a manner befitting the lineage of the instrument. The timpanist sits in the middle of the orchestra or band and carefully listening to the overall ensemble experience, places the notes correctly and with tone quality. Many times the excitement of the composition is left up to the timpanist because there is no other instrument in the ensemble capable of driving the tempo, producing the thunderous crescendo or playing a pianissimo barely audible to the audience. Much like the drum set player in the jazz band, the timpanist must, through imagination, do more with the part than is written on the page. That is not to say that improvisation is allowed, as in the drum set, but subtleties with dynamics and articulation are required if the timpanist is to do the job correctly. All the instruments in a musical organization are important but many times I have witnessed an unimportant role assigned to the timpani due mainly to the lack of understanding on the conductor's part or the lack of ability on the part of the timpanist. Both individuals must understand their responsibilities and perform in a musical and professional manner. This being done, the timpani will add the vitality needed to produce music.

Picture #1. Hand-tuned timpani

Picture #2. Dresden timpani

Construction

Timpani bowls are made of fiberglass, aluminum and copper which is the most popular. Copper produces the most resonance and is consider the standard for professional quality timpani. Many high schools use fiberglass bowls because of their durability and light weight, while aluminum is used when there is a shortage of copper or a light weight quality bowl is desired. Basically a kettledrum is a bowl upon which a head of either skin or plastic is placed. Hand tuned timpani bowls are placed in a cradle of wood and tuned by hand. (see Picture #1). The bowls for pedal timpani are placed into a cradle of metal to which a pedal is attached (see Pictures #2 & 3). The pedal mechanism is either attached to a spider on the underside of the bowl or there is a rod extending from the pedal mechanism which protrudes through a hole in the bottom of the bowl that is attached to a spider inside the bowl. In either case, the movement of the pedal forward or backward causes the spider, which is attached to tension rods running along the rim, to move the tension of the timpani head higher or lower which raises or lowers the tonal pitch. This seemingly simple procedure took centuries to perfect. Prior to the pedal mechanism all timpani were tuned by hand. About 1790, T-handles were placed through the rim and as they were turned clockwise or counter clockwise, the pitch either raised or lowered. In 1812, Gerhard Cramer, the Königliche Hofpauker (Royal Court Timpanist) in the Munich Court Orchestra, invented a rapid tuning device and in 1881 Carl Pittrich, Kapelldiener in the Royal Saxonian Orchestra, Dresden, Germany invented a tuning mechanism that used pedals much like our present-day timpani pedal mechanism. Between the years 1812 and 1881, there were several types of tuning mechanisms that were invented all proving inferior to the Pittrich model. Between 1911 and 1920, the Ludwig Drum Company in the United States with William F. Ludwig Sr. as founder, invented the Ludwig balanced-action pedal. This pedal is the most popular pedal mechanism used today. As a result of the inventions of Pittrich and Ludwig, we now have two types of timpani: the Dresden type characterized by its ratchet pedal mechanism and the Ludwig type characterized by its balanced-action pedal mechanism.

Picture #3. Balanced-action timpani

Bowls

The sizes of timpani bowls have changed over the years. Early bowls as described by Praetorius in 1619 were 17 1/2 and 20 1/2 inches in diameter. An early eighteenth century pair of timpani used in the Vienna Musikstrumenten-Sammlung in 1720 measures 22 1/2 and 24 3/8 inches in diameter. By the mid-nineteenth century, the sizes had increased to 24 and 26 inches in diameter. Today a set of five timpani range from 20 to 32 inches in diameter. The standard set of four timpani is 30, 28, 25 and 23 inches in diameter. Some companies now make a 26 and 29 inch diameter timpani which has replaced the 25 and 28 inch diameter drums. For a bigger sound, the timpanist may use a 32 inch diameter drum rather than a 30 inch diameter. For notes above a high A, the 20 inch diameter timpani is desired. Following is a range chart for timpani which indicates the best sounding notes on the drums. Notes higher and lower can be attained but their quality is not as good.

RANGE CHART

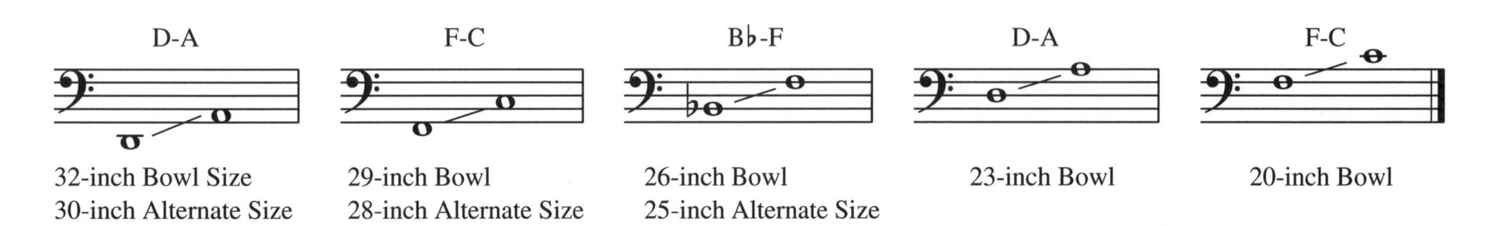

32-inch Bowl Size
30-inch Alternate Size

29-inch Bowl
28-inch Alternate Size

26-inch Bowl
25-inch Alternate Size

23-inch Bowl

20-inch Bowl

Timpani Mallets

There are numerous kinds of timpani mallets made by either the major percussion manufacturers or custom mallets made by individual timpanists or mallet manufacturers. Each mallet design has a distinct look and sound. Mallet handles can either be solid or hollow. Usually the solid handle is made from hickory wood and the hollow handle is made from bamboo or graphite. Sometimes a rubber grip covers that part of the handle where the hand holds it allowing for more comfort and relaxation. The felt on the playing end is usually piano felt and will come from either the United States or Europe. Minimally, the timpanist needs three basic pair of mallets — a general pair sometimes referred to as medium, a hard pair and a soft pair. With these three pair of mallets, the timpanist can play any part written for the timpani. Each of the aforementioned manufacturers will make a hard, medium and soft mallet. Quite often the selection of mallets is a result of the influence of the timpanists teacher who was, in turn, influenced by his/her teacher. The best timpani mallets to purchase are the ones made by individual timpanists or mallet makers. These individuals have taken great care in designing a mallet that produces a quality sound. Many times a mallet made by a percussion manufacturer is designed simply to be sold with the instrument without a great deal of concern for the sound it produces. These are usually inexpensive and readily available. On the other hand, custom-made mallets are quite expensive and not as readily available but well worth the expense and time to locate when considering that the sound produced will be superior. It is not uncommon for a timpanist in a major symphony orchestra to have ten or more pairs of timpani mallets. Each mallet is designed to produce a particular sound from very soft with no head contact sound, to ultra-hard for a percussive staccato sound. It is also quite common to see a double-ended mallet having wood on one end and felt on the other for quick changes from one sound to another. Many times a timpanist will make a pair of mallets to be used for a particular excerpt from the symphonic literature and use them only for that part. Discerning timpanists will take great care in selecting mallets, as they are an important element in the sounds they wish to produce.

Picture #4. Timpani Mallets with Rubber Grips

Hand Position

A natural and comfortable hand position is desirable for a smooth and relaxed playing technique. Holding the mallets correctly will assure complete relaxation throughout the wrist and arm. The player must feel that the mallet is an extension of the hand and should be held with no more firmness than if he were holding an egg. Basically, imagine that the hand is making the stroke and the mallet, which is extending from the hand, produces the sound. Both hands hold the mallets in the same manner and should have identical motions.

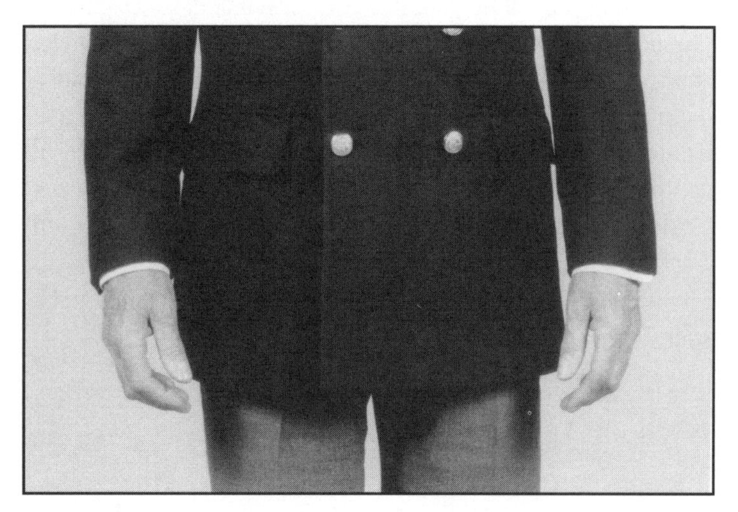

Picture #5 - Stand in a relaxed position with your hands at your side. Notice the natural curve of your fingers.

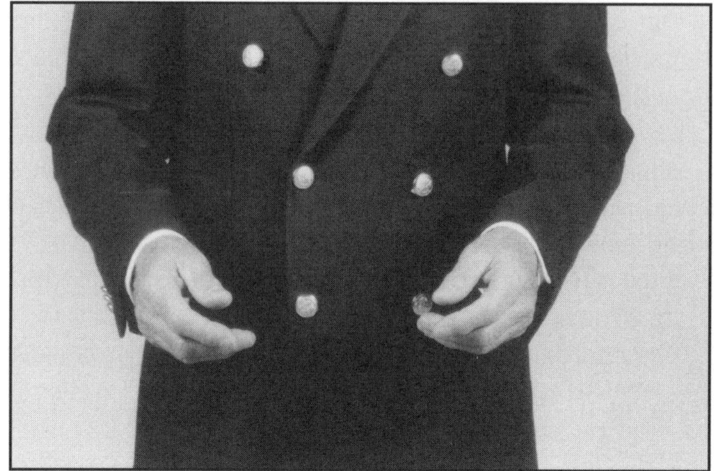

Picture # 6 - Extending your hands in front of you, the fingers should remain in the same position.

Picture #7 - Front view

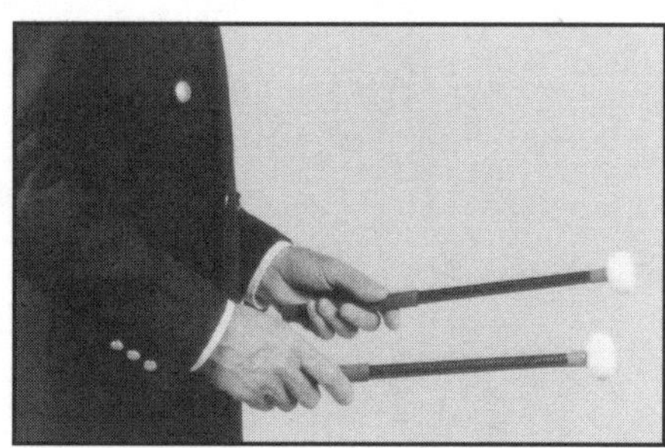

Picture #8 - Side view

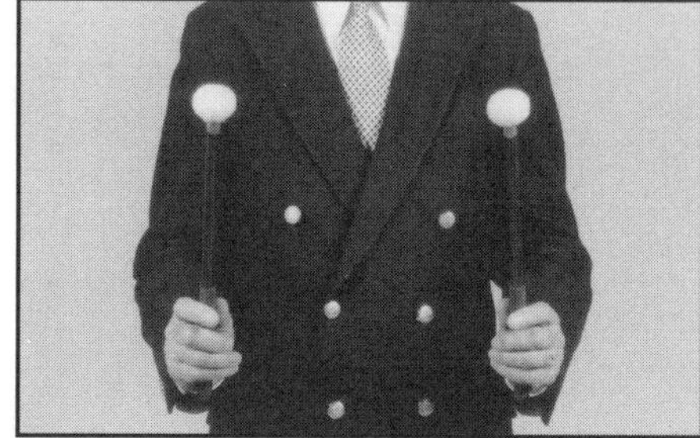

Picture #9 - Upright view

Pictures # 7-9 . Place the mallets in the hands taking advantage of the natural curve of the fingers. Allow the thumb to fall slightly to the left of center and place the index finger slightly ahead of the thumb. The second finger, thumb and index finger are the main controlling areas, while the last two fingers and fleshy part of the palm help control the mallets from moving to the right or left.

The thumb should be on the top or slightly to the inside of the handle much like it is when shaking hands with someone. Other techniques that require a more firm hand position do exist; however, these techniques are not as relaxed as the aforementioned technique and produce a harsher tone.

Playing Area

The proper playing area is approximately four inches from the edge of the bowl. To find this area, one can measure with a ruler but rather than use that procedure, strike the head in the center and witness that there is no tone. This is the node of the vibrating circle and produces a dull sound. Striking the head mid-way between the center and the edge of the bowl will produce more tone. Striking the head at the very edge will produce a thin tone. Somewhere between the mid-way point and the very edge is the best area to strike the head. To find that spot, let your ear be the judge. It will be approximately four inches from the edge of the bowl. Occasionally this area may be widened to accommodate loud playing. As a general rule, the mallets should be at least the width of a hand from each other when striking the timpani head.

Picture #10 - proper playing area for one drum

Picture # 11 - proper playing area for two drums

Picture #12 - widened area

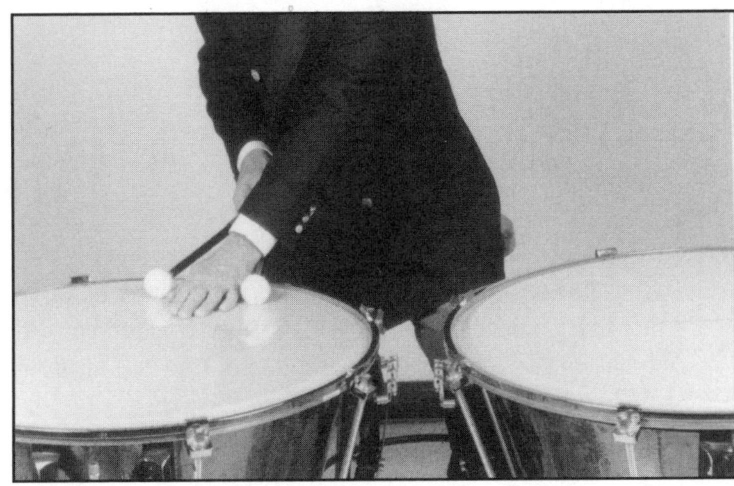

Picture #13 - hand between

Sitting/Standing

There is no rule for sitting or standing while playing timpani. There are however some basic considerations which will dictate which style to use. If you are tall, sit. If you are short, stand. If there is a lot of tuning while playing, sit. If there is no tuning while playing, stand. If two or four timpani are required, sit. If more that four timpani are required, stand. Pick the consideration that best fits your needs. Sitting on a high stool will assure ease of playing and tuning for most timpanists. Standing because of the necessity to bend at the lower back to perform does produce a bit more tension in the body and could, over the years, cause lower back problems. I prefer to sit because I can be more relaxed. Occasionally, when five or more timpani are required, I will stand.

Picture #14 - sitting

Picture #15 - standing

Tuning

Tuning the timpani to the correct pitches is of the utmost importance. One cannot play timpani if he/she cannot tune them. The two most important intervals used on timpani are the fourth and fifth. These intervals can be recognized by singing the first and second phrase of the Wagner *Lohhengrin* (Here Comes The Bride):

Tuning Continued

The tuning is done with the pedal found at the base of the timpani. Pushing the pedal forward raises the pitch and pushing the heel down lowers the pitch. It is a good practice to tune the timpani with your finger rather than the mallet. Two approaches to this procedure are:

APPROACH NO. 1 The finger flick or snap where the finger actually flicks or snaps the head causing it to produce a sound.

APPROACH NO. 2 The finger tap where the finger taps the head causing it to produce a sound.

Picture #16 - Finger Flick

Picture #17 - Finger Tap

Singing the desired pitch into the head, causing a sympathetic vibration, is also done to tune the timpani. In all cases, the ear must be close to the head in order to hear the pitch. Quite often timpani must be tuned while the orchestra or band is playing, therefore, it must be done as quietly as possible. If tuning must occur while the timpanist is playing a part, the foot must move the pedal the required distance because the player will not be able to listen to the new pitch until it is played. This technique can be learned with much practice and can be compared to the trombonist moving the slide the required distance to perform the new pitch. In either procedure, best results are attained when the desired pitch is approached from below. This will stretch the head as it reaches the note assuring that it will not change pitch when being struck with a timpani mallet. If the pitch is approached from above, the head will be relaxing as it reaches the note; consequently, there is a good chance that upon being struck with a timpani mallet, the head will relax more and become out of tune. In this case, it is necessary to go below the desired pitch and then move up to it. Remember that notes on the timpani sound best from mid-range to top-range. Always choose the drums which will produce the best sounding note. An example would be "C". It can be tuned on either the 28" or the 25" drum. It will sound much better on the 28" drum because it is at the top of the range. Consequently, the "C" on the 25" drum will not sound as well because it is at the bottom of the range. Sometimes it is necessary to tune a "C" on the 25" when "F"-"B♭"-"C"-"F" are the notes required; however, always consider the quality of the note when choosing the drum.

Tuning Gauges

Tuning gauges can be found on most timpani manufactured today. The gauges are meant to be an aid in tuning the timpani and not the final solution for tuning. The player's ear should be the sole dictator of the exact pitch; therefore ear training is a must if one is to become a timpanist. Tuning gauges were introduced with the Dresden timpani around 1881. Along with the new tuning mechanism the tuning gauges enabled the timpanist to make quick tuning changes not possible before.

It is this new technique that inspired Richard Strauss to write his timpani parts in *Till Eulenspiegels lustige Streiche* and *Salome*. Timpani gauges are most accurate when they are activated mechanically from the pedal mechanism such as on the Dresden timpani . A tuning gauge that is activated from the timpani head is not as accurate because of the uneven stretching and relaxing of the head. This gauge was quite popular with the early timpani made in the United States around 1920. Now all timpani manufacturers make a tuning gauge which is activated from the pedal.

Picture #18 - Dresden Timpani

Picture #19 - Modern Timpani

For the most part, all timpani parts should be tuned by the player using his/her ear to hear the pitch then transferring it to the timpani head with the timpani pedal; however, many timpani parts written for orchestras and bands today require that the timpanist rely heavily on the tuning gauges to tune the timpani. This is true because in today's music, it is not uncommon for the timpanist to have to tune while playing or possibly even tune to four new pitches in a brief rest. Gauges are a necessity in this case.

Getting Started

Timpani are tuned percussion instruments. Although the timpani heads are tuned for the range of each drum at the manufacturers, they frequently need re-tuning by the performer from time to time. This is not difficult and will help you to understand the drum and how it works.

STEP 1. Select a pitch on the piano and then with the timpani pedal move it up or down until you match that pitch on the timpani eg: 25" timpani select a D on the piano and match a D on the timpani.

STEP 2. Tap softly with a timpani mallet at each tension rod (these are the tuning rods which will raise or lower the pitch of the timpani head. They work the same as the tension rods on the snare drum). Listen carefully to hear that each tension rod area is the same as the pitch on the piano. If it is not, make an adjustment higher (clockwise) or lower (counter-clockwise) with the timpani tuning key.

STEP 3. Do this procedure for each drum. I suggest you match the following pitches to the following drums e.g.: 30" - G, 28" - A, 25" - D, 23" - E.

STEP 4. If the timpani heads are now in tune with themselves, you should be able to play notes in the entire range of each drum and have them in tune with themselves.

STEP 5. With the notes G-A-D-E, you are now ready to play the warm-up exercises in the next section; however, read the importance of warming up before you start to play.

No athlete will ever play a sporting event without warming up. No percussionist should ever practice or perform a concert without warming up. This simple but often over looked event will assure that the muscles involved in the performance of the desired skill will be relaxed and able to perform their duties. A slow simple beginning to the warm-up will make the most sense (e.g. single strokes with each hand at a medium volume, which then progresses into double strokes.) Each player should develop a warm-up study for themselves on each percussion instrument. This event should be practiced before etudes or concerts are played. How long this event should last will vary from day to day and should depend on how the player feels and how the sticks or mallets are responding. Once that magic feeling is achieved — only the player knows that —then it's time to get down to learning new music or performing the concert. Since playing percussion instruments involves the working together of many muscles, it is important that these muscles are not damaged. For one to pick up snare drum sticks and immediately start to play loud and fast, is assurance that eventually, if this procedure is continued over a long period of time, there will be permanent damage to the muscles. Not only muscles, but the joints of the wrist, hand and elbow are at risk with no warm-up period. Tennis Elbow and Carpal Tunnel are common problems caused by improper playing. Common sense is a key factor when doing any skill — IF YOU ARE HURTING WHEN YOU ARE PLAYING, SOMETHING IS WRONG AND YOU SHOULD STOP PLAYING.

A well thought out warm-up period will assure that the muscles are relaxed and the technical demands of the etude, solo or concert will be played at its best. Once the hands/arms feel relaxed, all concentration can be placed on the performance material and learning can take place. The mind is free to acquire new knowledge and not be focused on technical problems. After a good warm-up period and a concentrated practice session, the hands/arms should feel light and almost weightless. If they don't, then perhaps more warm-up is necessary. My advice to my students when they are practicing is: AT THE FIRST SIGN OF TENSION, SLOW UP THE TEMPO.

Warm-ups

A. SINGLE HAND

Following is a series of warm-up exercises to practice. I suggest that they be practiced starting SLOWLY with the single hand exercises and then progress to the others as the arms and hands feel comfortable. Eventually a progressive series of each warm-up page will evolve, which will become your warm-up routine. A good plan would be to set a metronome at a low number to start the exercises and the then progress to higher numbers as your technique improves.

B. HAND TO HAND

C. TRIPLETS

G-A-D-E
1
R L R L R L R L R L R L
2
R L R L R L R L R L R L
3
R L R L R L R L R L R L
4
L R L R L R L R L R L R
5
R L R L R L R L R L R L
6
R L R L R L R L R L R L
7
R L R L R L R L R L R L
8
R L R L R L R L R L R L
9
L R L R L R L R L R L R L R L R L R L R L R L R
L R L R L R L R L R L R L R L R L R L
10
R L R L R L R L R L R L R L R L R L R L R L R L
R L R L R L R L R L R L R L R L R L R
11
L R L R L R L R L R L R L R L R L R L R L R L R
L R L R L R L R L R L R L R L R L R L
12
R L R L R L R L R L R L R L R L R L R L R L R L
R L R L R L R L R L R L R L R L R L R

D. 16TH NOTE TRIPLETS

E. 32ND NOTES

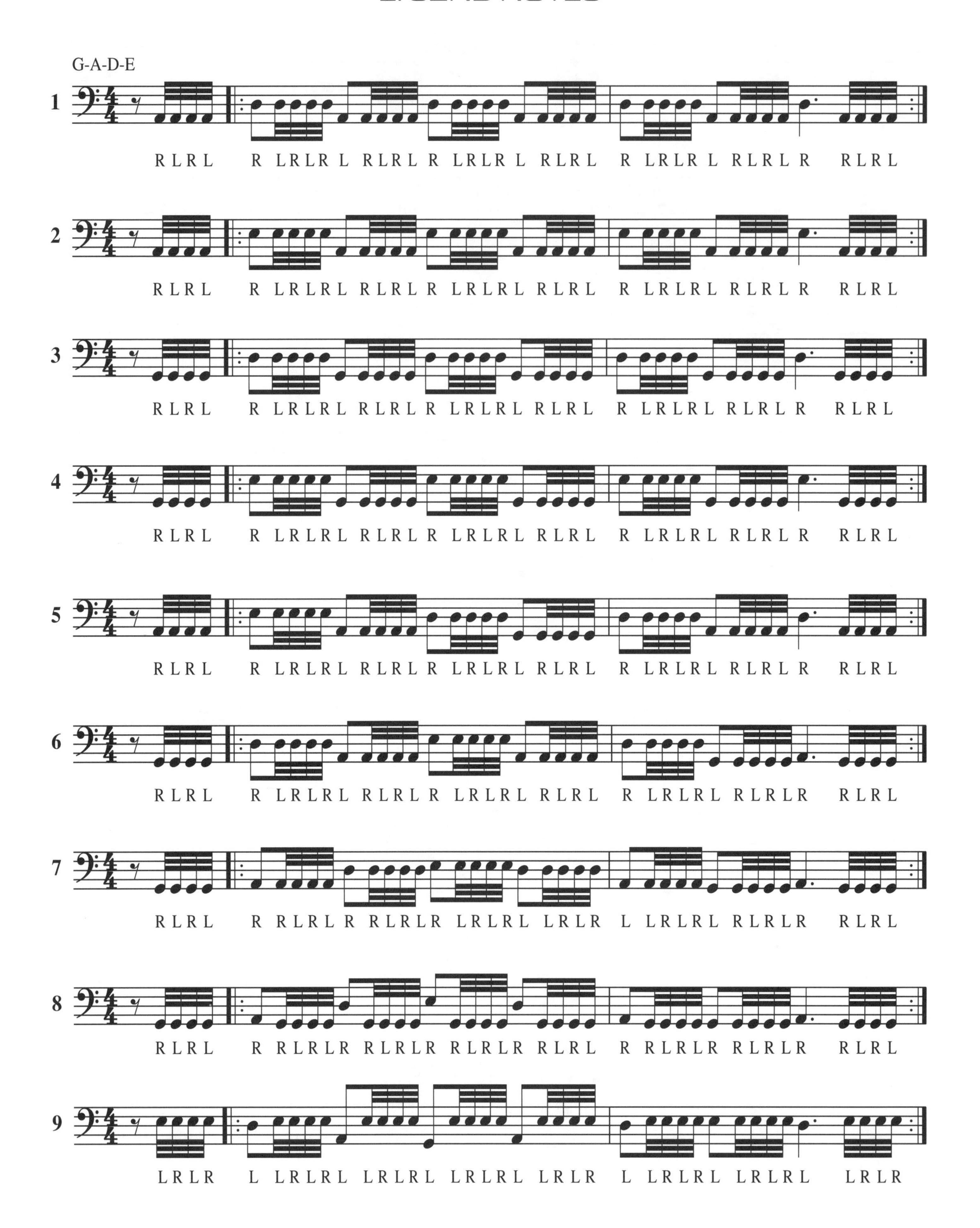
G-A-D-E
1
R L R L R L R L R L R L R L R L R L R L R L R L R L R L R L R L R L R L R L R L R L
2
R L R L R L R L L R L R L R L R L R L R L R L R L R L R L R L R L R L R L R L R L
3
R L R L R L R L L R L R L R L R L R L R L R L R L R L R L R L R L R L R L R L R L
4
R L R L R L R L L R L R L R L R L R L R L R L R L R L R L R L R L R L R L R L R L
5
R L R L R L R L L R L R L R L R L R L R L R L R L R L R L R L R L R L R L R L R L
6
R L R L R L R L L R L R L R L R L R L R L R L R L R L R L R L R L R L R L R L R L
7
R L R L R R L R L R R L R L R L R L R L L R L R L R L R L R L R L R L R L R L R L
8
R L R L R R L R L R R L R L R R L R L R R L R L R R L R L R R L R L R R L R L
9
L R L R L L R L R L L R L R L L R L R L L R L R L L R L R L L R L R L L R L R

F. MY FAVORITE WARM - UP

MY FAVORITE WARM-UP is an exercise that allows me to move around the drums, stretch my muscles and also get a feel for the placement of the drums. There is no meter to this exercise but you can see that a 3-2-2-3 pattern will enable you to move smoothly across the heads. Don't pound the mallets into the heads but allow them to drop on the head at the appropriate time. Place your feet on the floor, sit or lean on the timpani stool and rotate your body from the waist as you move around the drums. Start slowly and increase your speed as you feel comfortable. Practice at various dynamic levels.

G. CREATE YOUR OWN WARM-UPS (ON THE LINES BELOW)

Tone Production

Quality tone production is an absolute necessity when playing timpani. It is a known fact that anyone can hit a timpani head and get it to respond. I have heard this sound many times and it is not musical — IT IS NOISE. The proper method of striking the timpani is to lift the mallets from the head immediately upon coming in contact with it while always maintaining a relaxed hand position. This procedure is called LIFT and is done with the wrist and forearm. The player must always have the feeling that they are lifting the mallet from the head rather than hitting into it. LIFTING allows the head to vibrate freely and produces the best tone. Hitting into the head produces a percussive sound with little or no tone. There are different degrees of LIFT. The SLOW LIFT is achieved by using an arm motion which starts at the shoulder using upper arm, forearm and very little wrist. The mallet is then lifted from the head as if in slow motion. The results are a full rich tone with very little contact sound. The MEDIUM LIFT is achieved by using a motion that starts at the elbow and uses forearm and some wrist motion. The mallet is lifted from the head rather quickly. The results are a quality tone with the appropriate amount of articulation. This is the most common LIFT and is used for most timpani parts. The FAST LIFT is achieved by using a motion that starts at the wrist. The mallet is lifted quickly from the head. The results are a staccato tone which is appropriate when a short percussive tone is required.

Picture #20 - Slow Lift

Picture #21 - Medium Lift

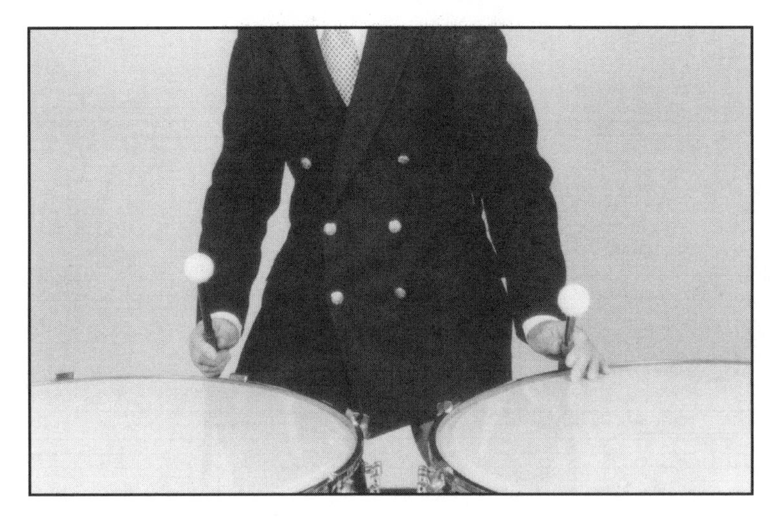

Picture #22 - Fast Lift

A. SLOW LIFT

The SLOW LIFT is accomplished by raising the arm above the timpani head and allowing the arm and mallet to drop, much as in a free fall, until it strikes the head. There is no wrist motion. Once the mallet strikes the head, the rebound is lifted from the head slowly and moved to the outside of the player's body. The sound produced has very little contact sound and is best used when playing long notes such as half and whole notes.

Following are examples to practice.

SLOW LIFT — use a full motion of the shoulder to the hand. Think long sounds with little attack. Musical style: Mozart.

B. MEDIUM LIFT

The MEDIUM LIFT is accomplished by lifting the mallet from the timpani head rather quickly immediately after the contact is made. There is considerable wrist action accompanied by a forearm motion which completes the LIFT. This LIFT is used for the majority of timpani playing and produces a clear articulated sound with depth and tone. A practice procedure to achieve the feel of this LIFT would be to place both mallets over the timpani head with the mallets heads held about chest level and wrists cocked. Strike the timpani head with one hand and immediately return to the starting position before the other hand strikes the head. This will give the player the feel of lifting the mallets from the head. Following are examples to practice:

MEDIUM LIFT — use a motion from the elbow to the hand. Think of a full sound with articulation. Musical style: Beethoven, Tchaikovsky.

C. FAST LIFT

The FAST LIFT is accomplished by lifting the mallets from the head very quickly with the wrist. The wrist does all the lifting and there is little or no arm motion. This produces a short articulated sound and is used when fast or staccato notes are required. This FAST LIFT can only be played for tempos which allow the player to lift each mallet from the head before the other mallet strikes. For tempos faster than that, the player must alternate hands and slightly tighten the grip on the sticks to produce an articulated sound.

Following are examples to practice:

Fast Lift — use a motion from the wrist to the hand. Think maximum articulation

Musical Style: Stravinsky, Bartók.

D. ETUDE FOR ALL LIFTS

Now that you have practiced the LIFT concept, ETUDE FOR ALL LIFTS is a test of your ability. A general rule would be that quarter notes are MEDIUM LIFT, eighth notes are FAST LIFT, half notes are SLOW LIFT. This all could change at the section ♩ = 72 and the presto section. Listen and perform the LIFT that produces the best tone.

E. LIFT ETUDES

The following eight timpani etudes are for two timpani and deal with the technique LIFT. They are written in an easy to difficult style and are intended to be exercises for study rather than solos for performance. There are no rolls so all note values are to be performed with the proper LIFT to assure that they sound their full value. Preceding each etude is a suggestion for mallet choice and musical intent.

LIFT ETUDE #1

GENERAL MALLETS - The tempo of quarter note equals 60 requires the whole notes and half notes to be performed with the SLOW LIFT and the quarter notes with the MEDIUM LIFT. Follow the dynamics carefully.

LIFT ETUDE #2

ERAL MALLETS - A MEDIUM LIFT should be used throughout this etude. This type of timpani writing is typical of timpani parts found in many earlier forms of music using timpani parts e.g. Mozart and Beethoven.

LIFT ETUDE #3

GENERAL MALLETS - A steady tempo is required in this etude along with a MEDIUM LIFT for the quarter and eighth notes and a FAST LIFT for the sixteenth notes. Be careful not to rush the sixteenth notes while performing the crescendo.

LIFT ETUDE #4

GENERAL MALLETS - This etude should have a feeling of a slow march and be performed with a MEDIUM LIFT. Always be aware of the dynamics and don't allo scendo to take place where it is not written.

LIFT ETUDE #5

GENERAL MALLETS - All dotted half notes are to be performed with a SLOW LIFT. The quarter notes are to be performed with a MEDIUM LIFT. Always keep the waltz feeling and pay attention to the dynamics.

LIFT ETUDE #6

GENERAL OR HARD MALLETS - If general mallets are used, the articulation would sound best with a FAST LIFT. If hard mallets are used, a MEDIUM LIFT could be used allowing the mallets to produce the articulation.

LIFT ETUDE #7

HARD MALLETS -This fast etude requires good control of both articulation and dynamics. Generally a FAST LIFT would work throughout but consider using a MEDIUM LIFT once in a while to change the character of the slower note values.

LIFT ETUDE #8

GENERAL MALLETS - Because the pitches are high for this etude and the tempo is fast, a general mallet would sound best. A relaxed FAST LIFT would help to bring out the articulation which will happen naturally.

Rolls

The long tone of the timpani is the roll. It must be even and as smooth as the long tone of any other instrument. Unlike the double stroke roll of the snare drum, the timpani roll is produced by rapidly alternating the hands in a single stroke roll style. The timpani roll does not have to be fast to sound correct. The essence of a good timpani roll is evenness not speed. Each pitch will dictate how fast the mallets must move. A low pitch with a loose head will require a slower roll than a high pitch with a tight head. Also, the hardness of the timpani mallet will affect the quality of the timpani roll. A soft timpani mallet will produce a full round sounding roll while a hard timpani mallet will produce a thin sounding roll with much contact sound. This very important technique must be mastered as the artistry of the player is often judged by the quality of the roll.

A. PREPARATORY ROLL ETUDES

PRACTICE PROCEDURE

1. Each tempo is to be performed over and over always keeping the notes equal to one another.
2. Practice at different dynamic levels.
3. Practice with both right lead and left hand lead.

B. ROLL NOTATION

Roll notation for timpani can be written a variety of ways depending on the time period of the music. Early music such as Mozart and Beethoven had rolls written like this:

Later in history composers such as Tchaikovsky wrote rolls like this:

Occasionally a composer uses 16th notes or 32nd notes to indicate a roll. If this style is used, it is because the tempo is fast enough to cause the notes to sound like a roll. If the tempo is slow, the 16th or 32nd notes will not sound like a roll but will be articulated notes which will compliment a particular part of the orchestration. Always check the tempo and do not assume that 16th notes and 32nd notes always mean a roll. Here are four examples to practice:

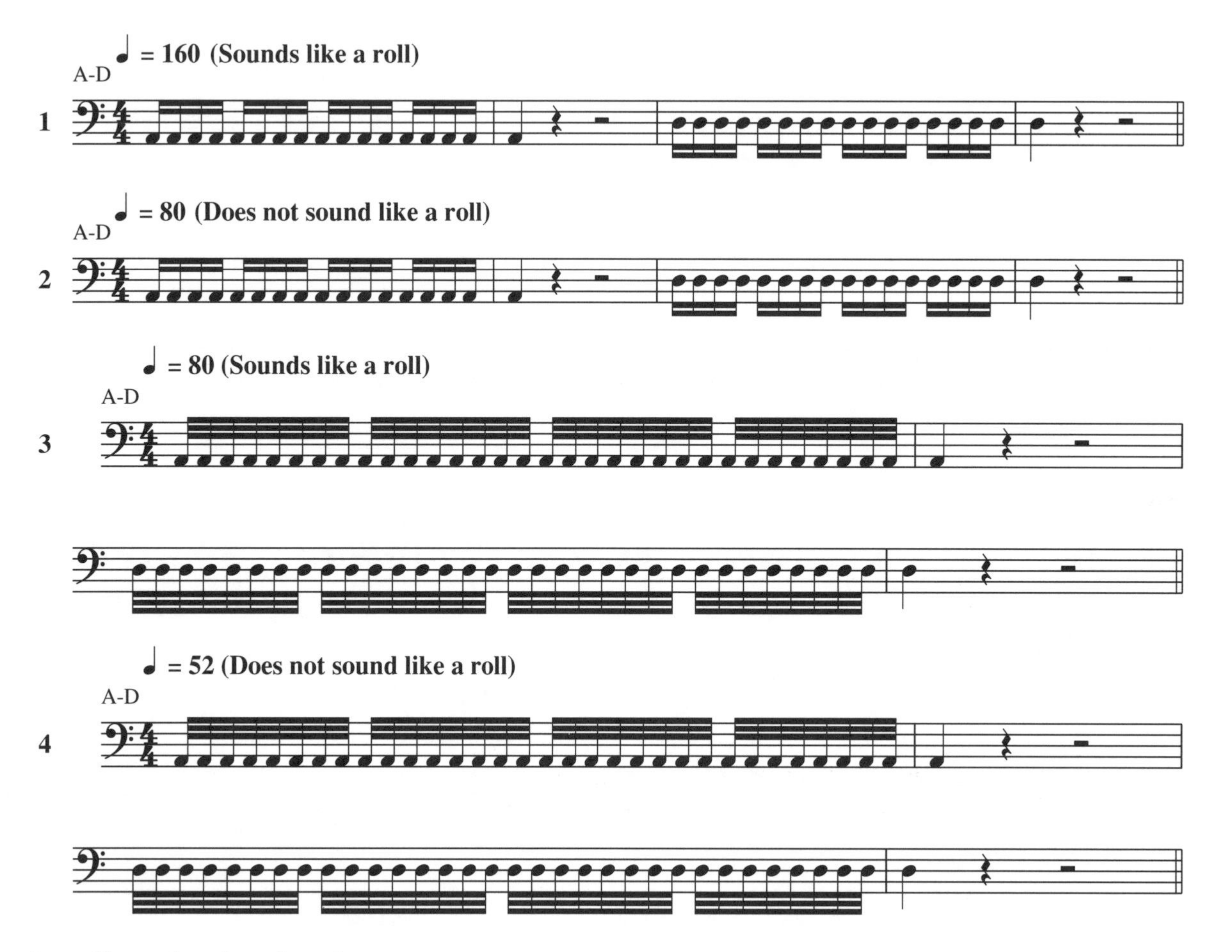

Following is a roll notation chart for reference:

5,6,7 and 8 will all sound alike. 5 and 6 could have slight pulsations for each note; however, there is no break in the roll.

Two different notations for the roll are used in this book. I have included both because they are typically found in timpani parts throughout the history of music. Becoming familiar with both kinds of roll notation will assure ease in reading timpani parts. In either case, the roll is traditionally tied to the release note unless the conductor or the music warrants a break before the release note. Following are some typical roll notations all with ended rolls:

Sometimes the following roll notation can be interpereted by extending the roll to the note following the tie. This would be done if there is a break in the music. Here are some examples:

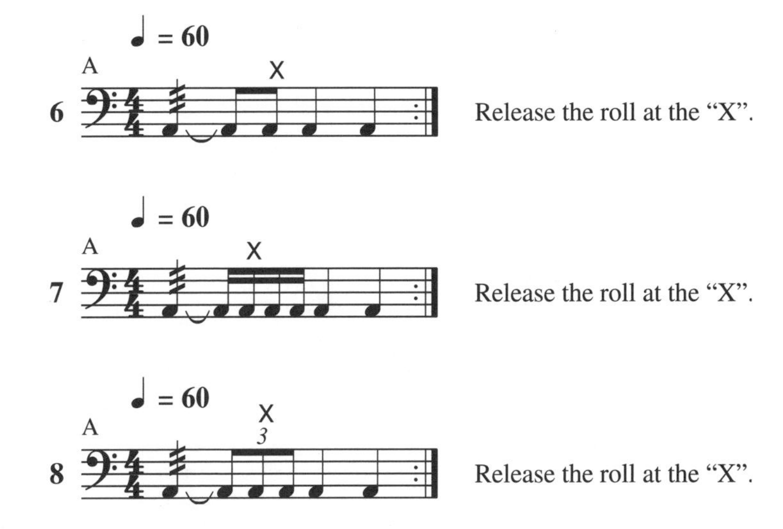

C. ROLL ATTACKS

The attack of the timpani roll is vitally important. It must have a clear beginning much like the door bell when pushed. A double or unfocused attack tends to obscure the rhythmic flow of the music. Regardless of the volume, the roll must start and continue as a smooth sound. Producing a good beginning requires that one mallet must start the head in vibration and the other mallet must enter within the sound produced. There is a primary attack and a secondary attack. Most rolls that have poor beginnings simply have two primary attacks. The best rolls are produced when one mallet starts from a higher position (primary) and the other mallet from a lower position (secondary).

Following are examples to practice:

For rolls that end with a rest, stop the mallets by lifting them quickly from the timpani head as you would stop your voice if you were yelling. There is no audible ending to this roll.

Repeat each line indefinitely and always focus on a good clean attack. For more practice, change the tempo and the pitches. On the repeat, start the roll on the opposite hand.

D. ROLL SPEED

The timpani roll can be compared to the long tone on a wind instrument or the smooth bowing of a string instrument. It is accomplished by the rapid alternation of the mallets in sympathy with the vibrations of the timpani head. A smooth even roll is the result of these two factors being coordinated. Since each pitch produces different head tension, the head vibrations will vary requiring different mallet speeds to produce the smooth roll. The skilled performer will make these subtle speed changes by listening and feeling the mallets working in sympathy with the head. The following will help to realize this concept.

You can readily hear that the high F does not sound like a roll but the low F does. High notes require a faster roll than low notes. Here is an example of several notes at various pitch tensions. Play them and you will feel and hear the difference.

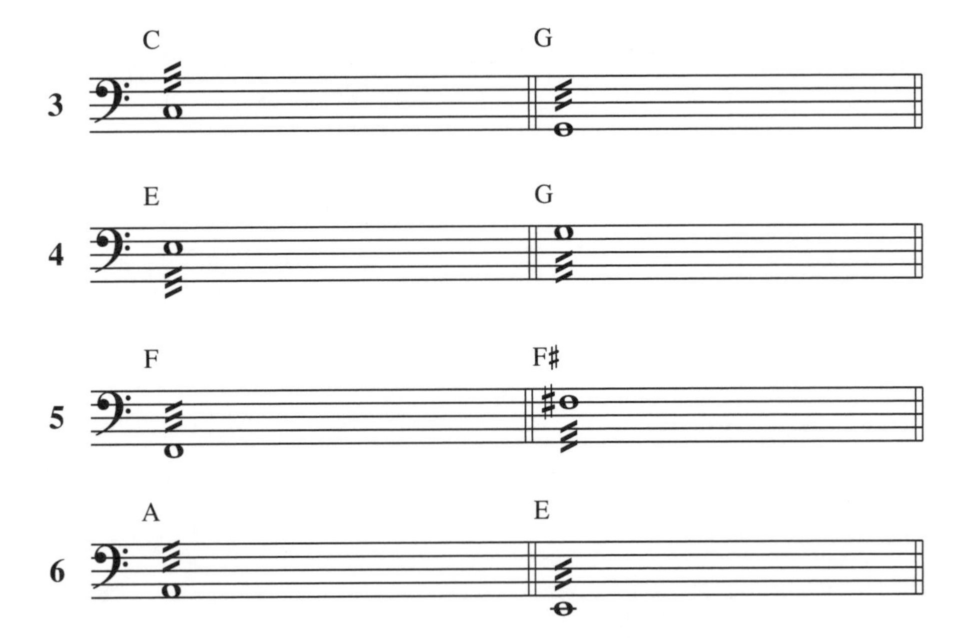

E. ROLL ENDINGS

The ending of the roll is a important as the beginning of the roll. If the roll has a single note following it, the single note must be executed with a definite clear sound. Lifting the mallet from the head at the completion of the roll produces this clear sound.

F. ROLL ENDINGS - OTHER DRUM

Rolls that end on other drums are also a concern of the timpanist. Many times the mallet required to complete the roll is not available at the precise moment and the ending is late or uneven. Following are examples of such rolls and how to execute them. In all cases, a rhythmic concept is used to accomplish this technique.

For longer rolls than are illustrated, the timpanist may play a non-rhythmic roll and apply the rhythmic pattern a beat or two before the note change.

G. CONTINUOUS ROLLS

Rolls that are continuous from one drum to another are yet another concern. There should be no break in the roll between drums. Again a rhythmic concept that will help produce this roll.

As a general rule, tie all rolls to each other or to single notes. This concept may change for certain musical situations or at the discretion of the conductor but, for good phrasing and musicianship, don't leave holes between rolls.

One important factor in performing rolls is to make sure that your body is over the area of performance. This will assure you of a relaxed upper body, attention focused on the area of performance, and a smooth roll.

H. FORTE-PIANO ROLLS

Forte-piano rolls are yet another concern for the timpanist. One mallet starts the head in vibration and the roll is started within the decay of the tone. High pitches require that the roll starts quickly after the attack. Low pitches require a later roll start. Following are examples to practice:

The START ROLL is an approximation, Let your ear determine when to start the roll.

I. ROLL ETUDES

ollowing roll etudes are to be performed after a good deal of time has been spent on perfecting the timpani roll. It is very important that there is equal control between hands and the roll has a full round sound. All rolls are to be tied to each other or to the note ending the roll. Lower notes will require a slower roll than higher notes. Let your ear help you decide the difference in roll speed between drums. Sometimes the same roll speed can be used for all pitches if the resulting sound is full and round. A GENERAL MALLET should be used for all the roll etudes; however, it is recommended that HARD and SOFT MALLETS be used from time to time as an experiment to realize the sound quality difference among the mallets.

ROLL ETUDE # 1

F and B♭ are pitches that produce full round sounds. A relaxed hand grip will assure that the full round sound is maintained.

ROLL ETUDE # 2

Play this etude with a steady tempo and follow the dynamics carefully.

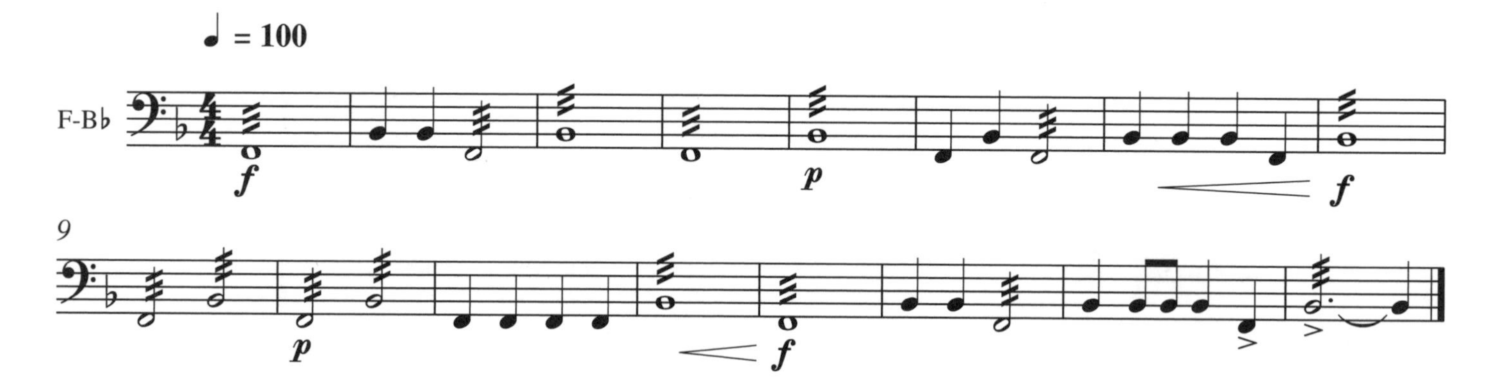

ROLL ETUDE # 3

Make sure that the rolls end precisely on the beat and watch the dynamics carefully.

ROLL ETUDE # 4

A measured roll will help to keep this etude in tempo; however, the hand speed must not be heard in the roll.

ROLL ETUDE # 5

Dynamics are important in this etude. Also the fast tempo will require some thought as to roll speed from drum to drum.

ROLL ETUDE # 6

Always keep the waltz feeling in this etude. Connect all rolls and play with musical tone in mind.

ROLL ETUDE # 7

This fast 6/8 etude will be challenging because all rolls are to be tied and dynamics followed carefully.

ROLL ETUDE # 8

This etude is all about forte-piano rolls. Execute them carefully and maintain the tempo.

ROLL ETUDE # 9

Three timpani are used in this etude which presents a movement consideration. Move the upper body in the direction of the drum which is being played. It will assure that the drum is played in time and with the proper quality sound.

ROLL ETUDE # 10

This etude is challenging. Four timpani are used and there is quick movement from drum to drum. Be careful to come off the rolls in time so the tempo is maintained. This etude is more like a solo and should be practiced only after the rolls are mastered.

ROLL ETUDE # 11

This etude reflects all concerns of rolling. It is difficult but if perfected, it will be assurance that all rolls found in most compositions will be playable. To understand the roll speed for the best sounding roll in this etude, certain measures have been selected and written in their proper notation with sticking on the following page. It is recommended that a slower tempo be used during the learning period of these measures. At first they will not sound like rolls but as the tempo is increased to the intended tempo, the roll will be controlled and sound smooth. REMEMBER TO TIE ALL ROLLS.

ROLL ETUDE # 11

PROPER HAND MOTION FOR SELECTED MEASURES

The top line shows the notation that appears in the etude. The line below shows the hand motion that will execute the roll properly at the tempo ♩ = 120. Use this as a guide to playing the etude in a musical manner.

Muffling

Muffling is done to prevent one sound from running into another. It is achieved by placing the hand on the timpani head, thus stopping the vibrations. It is wise to use the free hand to do the muffling; however, the muffling occasionally must be done with the same hand that strikes the drum. Both ways must be learned.

Picture #23 - free hand

Picture #24 - same hand

Always remember to keep the mallet in playing position when muffling. Muffling is not indicated in the part and must be used at the discretion of the player. Some simple rules of muffling must be understood as these equate to musicality:

RULE 1. muffle if the part is marked staccato

RULE 2. muffle if the rest after the note is more that two beats

RULE 3. muffle if the part goes from a loud dynamic to a soft dynamic

RULE 4. muffle if there is a cut-off at the end of the composition. It is also important to muffle all the drums after striking only one drum because sympathetic vibrations will cause the other drums to vibrate

A. MUFFLE-OPPOSITE HAND

Following are some exercises to practice to acquire a technique for muffling.

D. WHEN TO MUFFLE

Once facility has been achieved at muffling, a musical judgment must be made as to when to muffle in a composition. Not every rest needs to be muffled. The music, the conductor and the performer's experience are all part of the " when " to muffle. Following are four musical considerations regarding muffling.

Muffle at each rest. This is the proper way to interpret the music.

Do not muffle at each rest but allow the notes to sustain except for the last quarter note. This type of writing is typical of the Baroque and Classical period of music. The timpani and the trumpets must articulate the length of their notes the same.

Muffle at each rest. This is the proper way to interpret the music.

Loud to soft playing will also require a muffle.

Occasionally a series of quarter notes will sound clearer when the previous note is muffled as the new note is struck. This works best for dynamics of ***mf*** and above, solo playing and final cadences.

E. ETUDES

Following are four etudes to practice. The muffling will occur at the rest. Give each note its proper value and think like a wind player when executing the rhythms.

MUFFLING ETUDE # 1

MUFFLING ETUDE # 2

MUFFLING ETUDE # 3

MUFFLING ETUDE # 4

Cross Sticking

The technique of cross sticking is used to keep proper articulation in the playing when moving from one drum to another. The diameter of the timpani heads is large; therefore, single sticking is the best technique to use for good articulation. Doubling a mallet as in a paradiddle, RLRR - LRLL, will produce less than good articulation particularly when the head is in the lower range. The second of the doubled notes will sound weak compared to the first note. Also, this sticking produces a phrasing that is not desired in the music. The player should practice cross sticking which requires one mallet to move over the other and vice-versa.

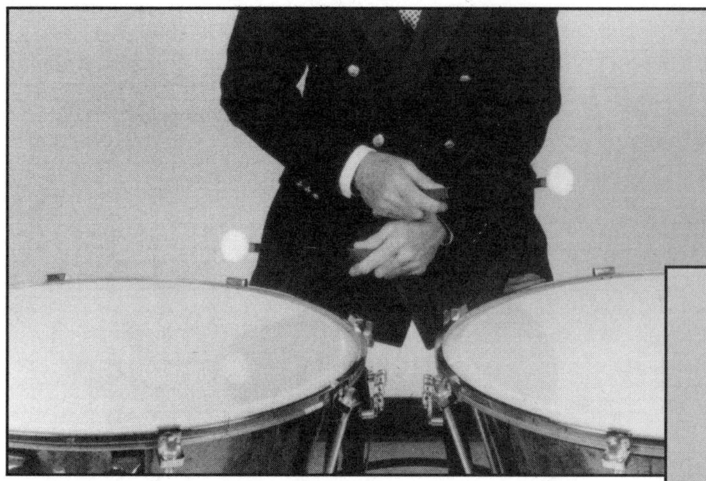

Picture #25 - right hand over left hand

Picture #26 - left hand over right hand

Picture #27 - wrong crossing technique.

The technique of shifting (moving one mallet out of the way of the other when moving from drum to drum) is also widely used but in my opinion causes a bit of tension in the playing that is not desirable; however, it does accomplish the same single sticking results as in cross sticking. There are times when a doubled note must be played in order to execute the part. In this case, it is the responsibility of the player to articulate the second note with the same articulation as the first.

A. RIGHT HAND CROSS

Following is a series of cross sticking exercises to practice. I suggest that they be practiced starting SLOWLY. Rather than stay with one series and complete it, I suggest that you move around in the different options and eventually a progressive series of cross sticking will evolve which will become your cross sticking routine. A good plan would be to set a metronome at a low number to start the exercises and then progress to higher numbers as your technique improves.

X = cross sticking

B. LEFT HAND CROSS

C. BOTH HANDS CROSS

D. ETUDES

CROSS STICK ETUDE # 1

Following are four cross sticking etudes to practice. The metronome marking indicates the desired tempo; however, a slower tempo will be fine for learning them and a faster tempo for a challenge.

CROSS STICK ETUDE # 3

* A double stop is playing two notes together. Unlike the flam in the snare drum technique, when playing a double stop, you produce two notes at the same time. To further understand this technique, play two notes together on the piano, and then play them the same way on the timpani.

CROSS STICK ETUDE # 4

E. COMBINATION ETUDES

The following four drum etudes are a continuation of all of the previous techniques and should be performed with a soloistic frame of mind. They are short in length and are written with a particular musical or technical concern in mind. The brief statement preceding each etude explains the intent of the etude and will provide immediate insight into what to work for.

COMBINATION ETUDE # 1

GENERAL MALLETS - This etude is much like a fanfare and serves to introduce the four drum etudes. Play with a full sound and stress dynamic contrast.

COMBINATION ETUDE # 2

GENERAL MALLETS - A melodic etude which must be well in tune for good results. Play with a relaxed hand grip and allow the drums to ring.

COMBINATION ETUDE # 3

HARD MALLETS - - A preparatory practice of this rhythm will prove helpful in attaining good results in this etude. Don't force the triplets but allow the hard mallets to produce the rhythmic patterns.

COMBINATION ETUDE # 4

GENERAL MALLETS - This is an etude in rolling. For best results, there should be no break between rolls when moving from one drum to another. Follow the dynamic contrast very carefully.

COMBINATION ETUDE # 5

GENERAL MALLETS - A seemingly easy etude develops into a difficult one. Follow the accents and cross-sticking very carefully. Don't set the tempo faster than indicated just because the first eight measures are easy.

COMBINATION ETUDE # 6

HARD MALLETS - This etude is melodic all the way. It should never get heavy in sound even though the dynamic of forte is reached. When double stops are played, the right hand is the melody and the left hand is the accompaniment.

COMBINATION ETUDE # 7

GENERAL MALLETS - The feeling of 2+2+3 should always be stressed. When playing the double stops, always stress the moving line. If both hands move in the same direction, there should be equal volume between hands.

COMBINATION ETUDE # 8

GENERAL MALLETS - Move quickly and evenly off the rolls. Always end the rolls that are tied. Leave no holes between the triplet rolls and count them carefully.

COMBINATION ETUDE # 9

GENERAL MALLETS - This etude is melodic and should never get too heavy. The rhythmic modulation from 12/8 to 4/4 to 12/8 should be smooth. The preceding measure before the meter change will establish the new tempo.

COMBINATION ETUDE # 10

GENERAL MALLETS OR HARD MALLETS - This etude has drama, melody and technique. It is the culmination of the four drum etudes. Follow the dynamic and sticking carefully. Consider this etude a solo.

15
X
X
X X
ff
R L R
L R L
R L R L R L R L
p
17
X
X
R L R L R L R L R L R L
20
ff L R R L
L R R L
L R
22
X
R L R L R L R L L R R L L L R
L R R L L L R R
25
L R L
p ff
27
X
R
R R L R
p ff
29
3
rit. X
p L
R L L R
ff L R
R L R L
31
a tempo
rit.
sfz
L
p ff
L R L L
R
fff

Pedaling

The ability to pedal timpani rapidly and accurately is a technique that can be learned with practice. Several factors are involved:

1. **The ability to hear the interval before it is tuned.**
2. **The physical feel of the foot on the pedal.**
3. **Confidence.**

The ability to hear the interval in the mind can be learned by singing the original pitch, thinking the new pitch and then singing it. Play a note on the piano, sing the note, think the new note, sing it and finally check it on the piano. With practice, perfection can be attained.

The physical feel of the foot on the pedal means that the foot has the sensitivity to feel or measure movement. Each interval has a certain degree of movement in inches. A half step will require less movement that a whole step. A third will require less movement than a fourth etc. With practice, one can feel intervals with the foot. Many times contemporary music requires tuning changes while playing other drums.

Confidence is a psychological characteristic which is enhanced by attaining some degree of accuracy at a skill. The more accuracy attained, the more confidence one acquires. As one is able to sing the new pitch correctly and tune it on the timpani, one's confidence is increased. Confidence will enable the performer to " go after " the new pitches with no apprehension. This ability will prevent the frequent pre-tuning of the timpani which often causes the performer to miscount measures and make wrong entrances. Having the confidence to pedal timpani accurately also gives the performer the feeling of playing a musical instrument rather then several pre-tuned drums.

The procedure for pedaling timpani is as follows: think the new pitch, the pedal and the mallet move simultaneously and the new pitch is played. There should be no glissando between pitches. Think of the trombonist moving the slide and move the pedal in the same fashion. A subtle movement of the pedal may be necessary to correct the pitch if it is not accurate. With practice, scales and melodies can be performed.

Intervals

An interval is the distance between any two pitches. There are several intervals to a scale and can be recognized by their whole steps and a half steps. Following are C, F and G Major scales with the whole steps and half steps clearly marked, as well as the most used intervals.

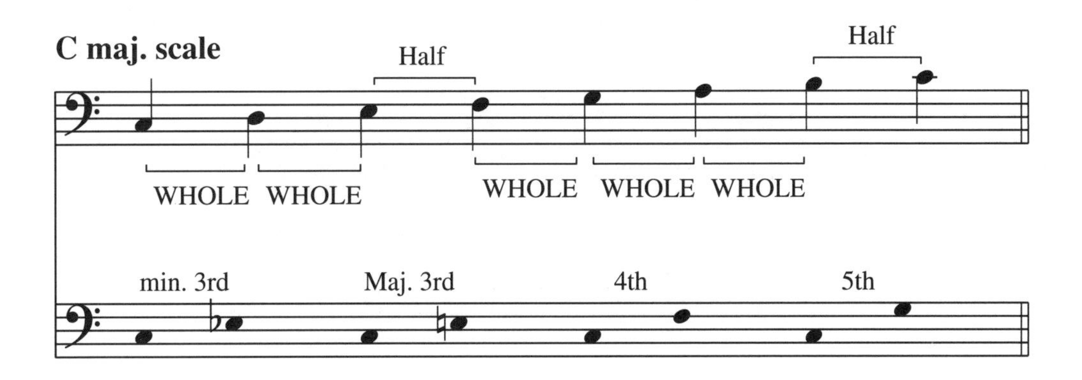

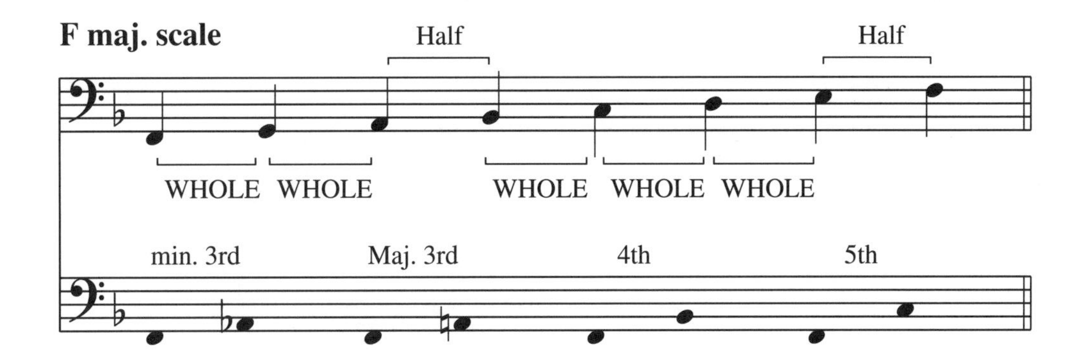

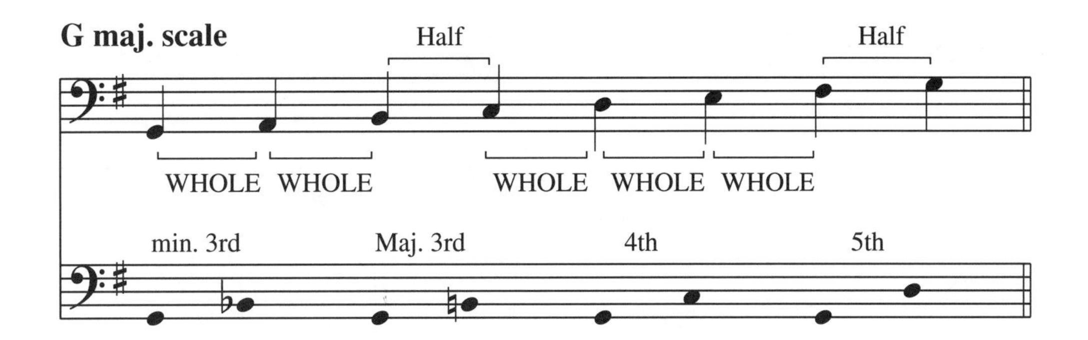

Exercises

The following interval exercises will help to establish an accurate pedaling program. Play the exercises at the piano or mallet instrument and listen to the notes. Once the notes are familiar to you, try playing them on the timpani. Use one mallet and do not play too loudly. It may help to actually play a glissando between the notes at first to get the feel of the pedal movement; however, the ideal sound is without glissando. A glissando is performed by slowly raising or lowering the pitch to another pitch. This is done on the timpani by pushing the pedal forward or downward with the foot on the timpani pedal.

A. HALF STEPS

EXERCISES FOR THE LEFT FOOT

EXERCISES FOR THE RIGHT FOOT

B. WHOLE STEPS

EXERCISES FOR THE LEFT FOOT

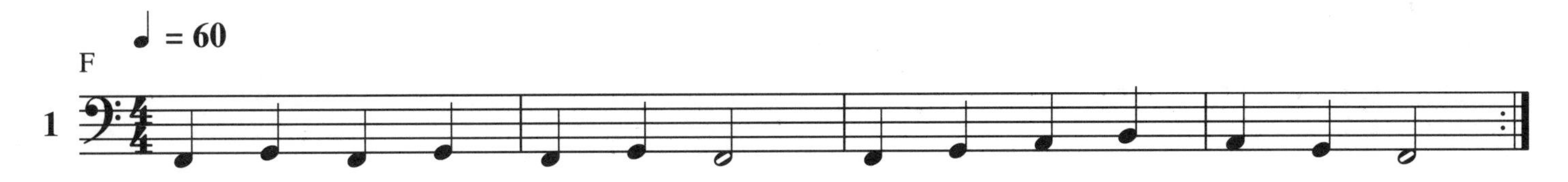

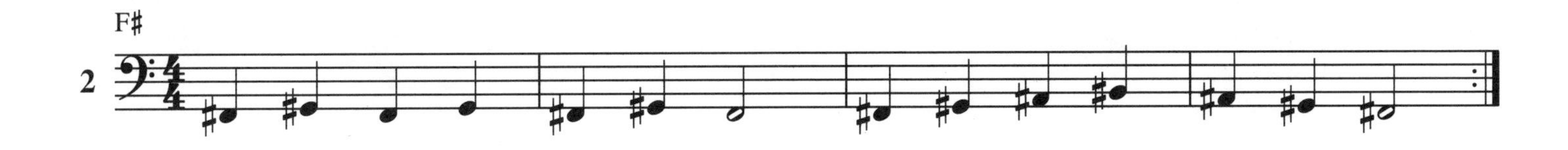

EXERCISES FOR THE RIGHT FOOT

C. MINOR THIRDS

EXERCISES FOR THE LEFT FOOT

EXERCISES FOR THE RIGHT FOOT

D. MAJOR THIRDS

EXERCISES FOR THE LEFT FOOT

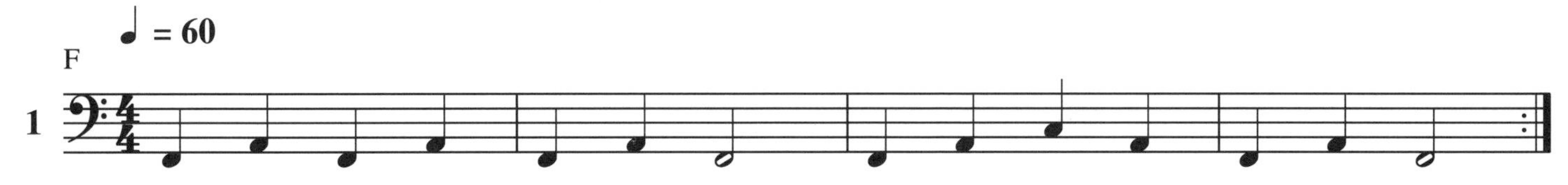

EXERCISES FOR THE RIGHT FOOT

E. PERFECT FOURTHS

EXERCISES FOR THE LEFT FOOT

EXERCISES FOR THE RIGHT FOOT

F. PERFECT FIFTHS

EXERCISES FOR THE LEFT FOOT

EXERCISES FOR THE RIGHT FOOT

G. SCALES FOR BOTH FEET

H. MELODY PRACTICE

The following short pedaling melodies are to be practiced after the interval exercises are more familiar. Two timpani are required and remember to place the **left foot** on the **large drum** and the **right foot** on the **small drum.**

MELODY PRACTICE LEFT FOOT

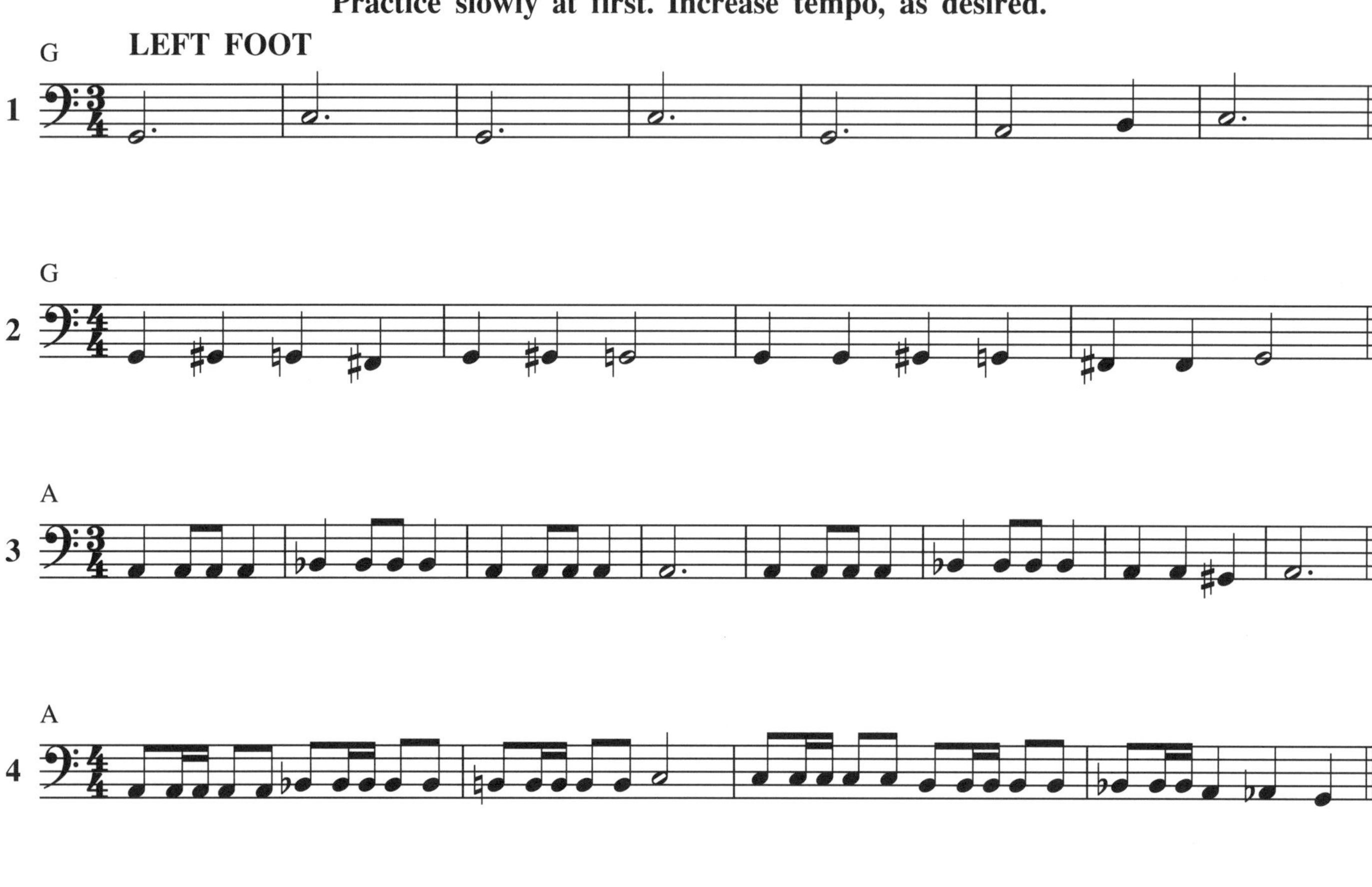

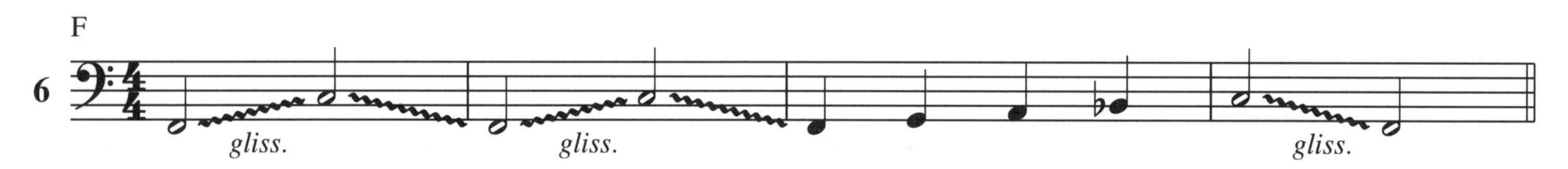

* To play a glissando (gliss.) strike the 1st note and move the pedal to slide to the second note, strike the second note on the appropriate beat.

MELODY PRACTICE RIGHT FOOT

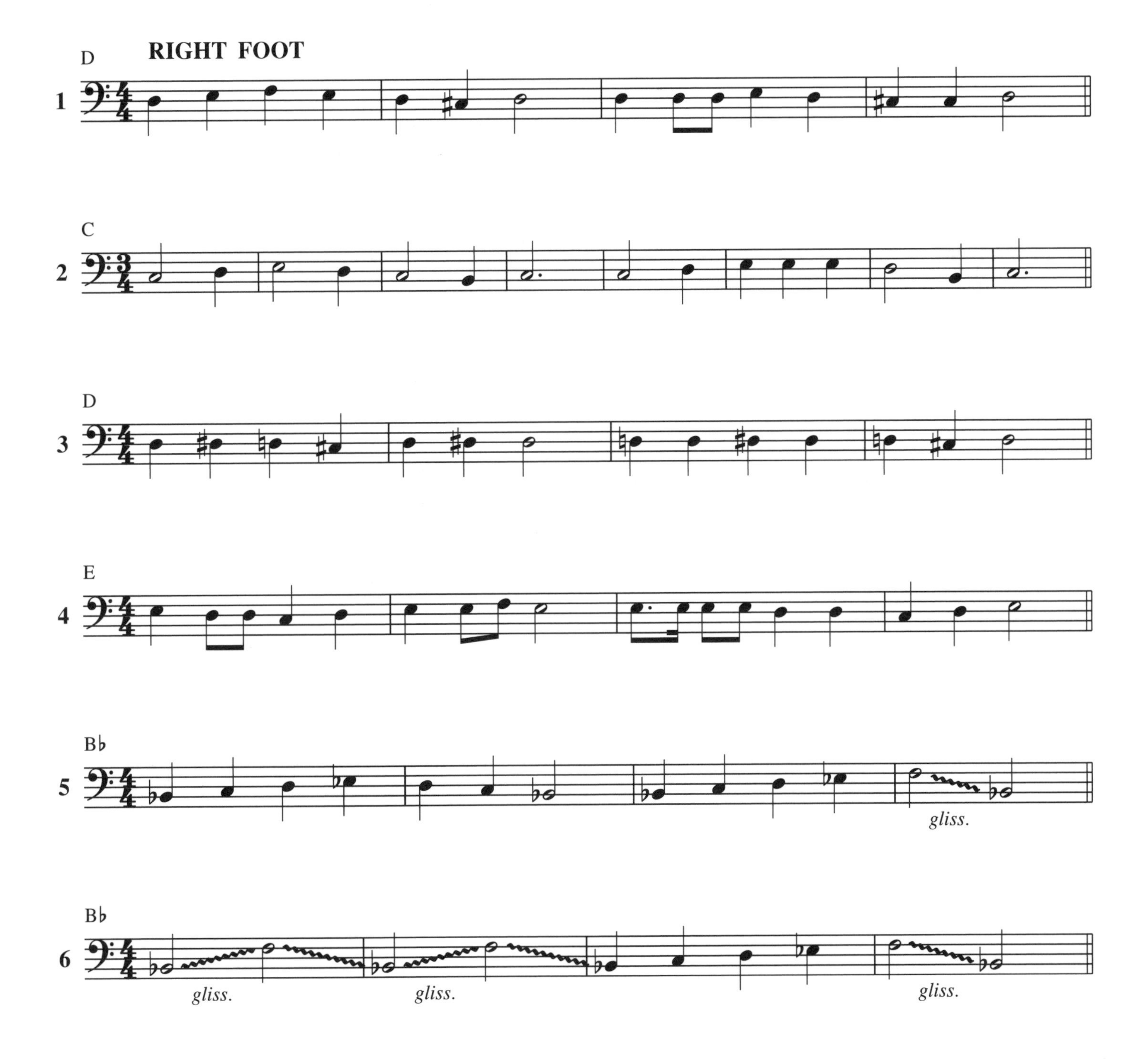

MELODY PRACTICE BOTH FEET

Brackets are used to indicate when to pedal each drum. e.g.: [ ]

I. PEDALING SOLOS

The following short solos are to be practiced after there is a thorough knowledge of the interval exercises and melodies. There are no brackets used to indicated the pitch changes for the three following etudes. Most timpani music is written this way and it is the player's job to indicate the pitch changes they feel works best for them; therefore, it is up to you how you want to indicate the pitch changes for the etudes. Following are some examples of how timpanists mark their parts:

PEDALING EXERCISES

PEDALING SOLO # 1

PEDALING SOLO # 2

* Feet on the two highest drums.

PEDALING SOLO # 3

* Feet on the two highest drums.

Contest, Festival and Recital Solos

The following twelve timpani solos are written to explore various timpani techniques that have been discussed in previous sections of the book. Each solo is written in a soloistic manner and not as an etude; therefore, each one could be used for recitals or festivals. A brief statement before each solo regarding musical intent and mallet choice will help to perform it with full understanding.

This section is a culmination of all of the material presented in this book. Be sure to read the introductory statement before playing each solo. If any of the techniques incorporated are presenting performance problems, go back to the relevant section and practice the technique in an isolated manner.

Although these solos pose technical demands, your overall goal is to perform them in the most musical manner possible. Master the technical aspects first so when performing, your focus can be on the musical aspects.

Enjoy!

SOLO # 1

RAL MALLETS - This solo is concerned with ...us LIFTS. The opening melody contains the medium lift, fast lift and slow lift. Throughout the solo these lifts keep appearing and it is the responsibility of the performer to execute them with quality sound. Keep a relaxed hand grip at all times and the solo will sound musical.

SOLO # 2

GENERAL MALLETS - A steady tempo must be maintained throughout this solo which demands that the eighth note be constantly in mind; otherwise, the tempo will have a tendency to rush. The medium lift is the primary technique used to execute this solo. Follow the dynamic contrast with a musical line in mind.

SOLO # 3

GENERAL MALLETS - The opening twelve measures should be executed with precision allowing all the sixteenth notes to have a quality sound that is clear and musical. A relaxed hand grip will assure that this is attained. Follow the dynamics carefully and make sure that the melody line is clearly heard over the repeated notes. Always play with LIFT in mind.

SOLO # 3 (CONT.)

SOLO # 4

HARD MALLETS - The fast lift is the technique used to execute this solo. Careful attention must be directed to keeping the mallets low and the dynamic of *sempre p* maintained. Always direct your attention to the pitch change when it happens and focus on that drum. Read ahead so that the changes will be smooth and the tempo will be maintained.

SOLO # 4 (CONT.)

33
f
X
37
X
X
R R L
41
45
p
49
f
X
53
L
R
56
R
p
59
63
X
ff
67
X
X
X
71
X
X
X = cross sticking
2:25

SOLO # 5

SOFT MALLETS - It is important that all rolls be tied to each other and to ending notes. The flow of the solo must be maintained while concentrating on smooth rolls. The tempo of ♩= 72 will establish a rhythmic pulse which can be worked into the roll for a smooth performance. The dynamic contrast is quite important for the musical content of this solo.

SOLO # 6

HARD MALLETS - Every note value must be executed with great care in order for this solo to be effective. The muffling procedure (same hand or other hand) must be thought out quite well and always maintained to keep a steady tempo. Dynamics and accents are extremely important to this solo.

SOLO # 7

HARD MALLETS - This solo is all about mixed meter with a steady eighth note. The technique used for the best execution is between a medium and a fast lift. The hard mallets will help maintain clarity; therefore, a relaxed hand grip will produce a quality sound. Pay attention to the dynamic contrast and always keep a steady eighth note.

SOLO # 7 (CONT.)

57
f
p
64
f
73
81
p
f
88
p
96
p
f
103
111
ff
117
dim. to end
122
128
l.v.
pp
2:10

SOLO # 8

GENERAL OR HARD MALLETS - When performing this solo keep in mind that the grace notes should never interfere with the flow of the written rhythm. They are embellishments and elongate the note but do not change its value. They should be played as fast as possible and be subordinate to the main note.

SOLO # 8 (CONT.)

SOLO # 9

GENERAL OR HARD MALLETS - This solo is all about cross sticking. Keeping the mallets low will assure that cross sticking will be executed smoothly and the rhythm will be even. Always lean in the direction of the cross sticking so that the moving mallet will land with the correct intensity. Follow the dynamics carefully.

SOLO # 9 (CONT.)

59
ff
p cresc.
65
71
f
77
p
83
f
89
95
ff dim.
101
p cresc.
107
112
p cresc. to end
118
125
2:00

SOLO # 10

GENERAL MALLETS - When performing this solo, think like a trombone player. There should not be a *glissando* between pitch changes and when a *glissando* is written, the ending note is to be struck. There should always be a waltz-like feeling to this solo. A medium lift would be perfect to realize the musical content of this solo.

SOLO # 11

GENERAL MALLETS - Double stops on timpani are to be performed like double stops on the piano. There should never be any grace note feeling and always focus on the pitch change rather than the repeated note. A medium lift would be perfect for this solo.

SOLO # 12

GENERAL MALLETS - This solo is all about control. The repeated 16th notes are not to be articulated like a snare drum part but are always to be as soft as possible. The accented notes are not to be loud but just above the level of the 16th notes. It is advisable to always move the body as well as the hand in the direction of the accented notes assuring that the notes will be played with a quality sound. The suggested tempo is playable but a slower tempo will also produce good results.

SOLO # 12 (CONT.)

40
43
46
49
52
55
58
61
64
67
70
73
76
79
81
repeat ad lib.
morendo
4:30

Hints To The Timpanist

1. Three different types of mallets are needed - hard, medium (general) and soft.
2. Hold the mallets with no more firmness than if you were holding an egg.
3. The playing area is four inches from the edge of the bowl.
4. Always play with a lift.
5. Tune from below the desired pitch.
6. Tune with your fingers and play with the mallets.
7. Notes on the timpani sound best from mid-range to top-range.
8. The essence of a good timpani roll is evenness, not speed.
9. Cross sticking is used to keep a rhythmic pattern even, not to "show off".
10. Always keep the mallets in playing position when muffling.
11. Keep the mallets covered when not in use; this will protect the felt end.
12. Keep timpani heads in tune with themselves by making sure the pitch is the same at each tension rod.
13. Use the best plastic heads available.
14. Keep all mechanical moving parts well lubricated.
15. Use tuning gauges as a guide, not as the final result.
16. COPERTO means to place a small cloth on the timpani head to muffle the sound.
17. If two drums are used in a set of four, muffle the unused drums so there is no sympathetic vibration.
18. Sit on a high stool for relaxation and ease of tuning.
19. Leave timpani heads in mid-range when the drums are not being used.
20. TIMPANI - Italian PAUKEN - German TIMBALES - French TIMBALS - Spanish